THE AUSTRALIAN EXPAT SURVIVAL GUIDE

An Essential Guide To Your Financial Well-Being

Mike Reynard

GRANDDADS INVESTMENTS LTD

<u>Personal Financial Services for Australian Expatriates</u>

AuthorHouse™ UK
1663 Liberty Drive
Bloomington, IN 47403 USA
www.authorhouse.co.uk
UK TFN: 0800 0148641 (Toll Free inside the UK)
UK Local: 02036 956322 (+44 20 3695 6322 from outside the UK)

Because of the dynamic nature of the Internet, any web addresses or links contained in this book may have changed since publication and may no longer be valid. The views expressed in this work are solely those of the author and do not necessarily reflect the views of the publisher, and the publisher hereby disclaims any responsibility for them.

Any people depicted in stock imagery provided by Getty Images are models, and such images are being used for illustrative purposes only.
Certain stock imagery © Getty Images.

This book is printed on acid-free paper.

ISBN: 979-8-8230-8415-4 (sc)
ISBN: 979-8-8230-8416-1 (e)

Library of Congress Control Number: 2023915032

Print information available on the last page.

Published by AuthorHouse 08/16/2023

authorHOUSE®

PREFACE

It's been years now that each time I arrive at Changi Airport I draw a genuine sigh of relief and think 'I'm home.' A scary thought for and Englishman, really. I arrived in Singapore at the age of 26, a young investment advisor in search of adventure, obtained a taste for the expatriate lifestyle and have never looked back.

During this time I have been a financial adviser to the international expatriate communities in the Middle East and the far east, and have been fortunate enough to work in Abu Dhabi, Hong Kong, Jakarta, Malysia, and Singapore.

Over the past 25 years I have met and interviewed thousands of expats from all walks of life about financial situations and aspirations. Naturally, when you talk to people about their finances, you also find out about (and must take into consideration) many aspects of their personal lives.

This book is a summary of some of the invaluable information I have collected along the way – not just about financial matters, but the unique life experiences that go hand in hand with the expatriate lifestyle.

Much of the content of the following chapters are based on real – life experiences of expatriates who have unknowingly succumbed to the many traps and pitfalls that lie in wait beyond the comforts of their homelands.

The expatriate lifestyle is one that can expose you to some nasty situations, which you are often unprepared for. As an expat, you don't have the same family, social, cultural, and legal support systems that you are used to. This can lead to stress and confusion when it comes to facing a difficult situation or making important decisions. And the outcome of these decisions can continue to affect your life, long after you have repatriated. So, it's important to always keep the big picture in mind.

Also, it's easy to become complacent because of the extra salary and the cushioned lifestyle your company has set up for you. Everything is taken care of. The housework, the car, the kid's education… so we forget about 'real life' back home and put off or ignore planning for your eventual repatriation – which will arrive one day, sooner or later.

So, the aim of this book is to help expats of all nationalities, both old and new, to avoid the many traps they could find themselves in. With some simple forethought and planning, common mistakes can be avoided, saving you thousands of dollars in lost revenue via overpaid taxes, inadequate employment contracts and bad advice from the con men and sharks that do exist out there. While my recollections and cartoon illustrations are sometimes humorous, some of the real-life situations you will read about are heart breaking, yet nevertheless true.

I also want to spread the good news that there are numerous financial benefits available of offshore investment opportunities, offshore banking facilities, and legal tax loopholes which you can access only while you are living and working as an expatriate.

The expatriate contact is a wonderful opportunity for people to enhance their own (and their family's) financial status, while seeing the world and meeting people from many different cultural backgrounds. It will expose you to cultures and traditions that one would not ordinarily see in one's hometown. It's an opportunity for your children to study in top international schools and for the family to regularly holiday in exotic locations that would normally be on the other side of the world and therefore probably inaccessible. It is certainly a life-enriching opportunity, which when planned properly, can be a wonderful adventure and can set you up for the rest of your life.

I hope you enjoy this guide. It is the result of 25 years living overseas and a rewarding career as a financial advisor. Although my time as an expat will one day come to an end, I can look back and say that I've met many interesting people and heard some amazing true stories. In short, I have enjoyed every minute of it. I hope your stint overseas is just as fulfilling and financially rewarding.

CONTENTS

So, you're fed up with the cold winters and short summers in your hometown. You need a change and you've got the urge to travel. Perhaps you and your partner have decided that enough is enough. Job prospects aren't that good and the idea of travelling to an exotic location beckons. You do your sums and realise you will pay a lot less tax than you do now, and at the same time have the opportunity to earn more money, pay off the credit card, and get rid of that millstone of a mortgage. It all sounds too good to be true!

You know some friends who have worked overseas and have seen how their lifestyle and standard of living have vastly improved, although they are in the same professional league as you are. And the opportunity of giving the kids a better start with broader horizons and a good education (hopefully paid for by the company you will be working for) far outweigh the alternative of overcrowded and underresourced schools at home.

So, you start to make some inquiries. Finally, you are offered a job in an exotic location. You and your partner begin to gather together some information by visiting the local bookshop and the website of the country you will be travelling to. After checking all this out, you look at each other and say, Let's go for it! After all, it's only a few years of our working lives. And just think of the amount of money we can save!'.

You then arrange to let or, in some cases, sell your home (the pros and cons of this are covered in chapter 6: The housing trap). However, there are many things to consider before boarding your flight. Below are some pointers to make sure you arrive with a soft landing rather than a hard bump.

Getting your contract right

Always negotiate your contract before leaving home. Once there, you won't have the bargaining power to change things you don't like. Also, don't feel pressured to take the first offer, no matter how desperate you are to get going. In short, before leaving, make sure you are satisfied with your future arrangements by investigating the following terms:

- Income tax: Ask about the rate you are liable to pay in the country you will be working in and who is responsible for paying it? In most cases you will be liable, but these days more and more companies are offering to cover their employees' income tax liabilities. So, whenever possible, ask your company to pay and make sure this is included in your contract.
- Immigration laws: How these will affect the terms of your employment and your dependants.
- Housing allowance: Always compare this with the standard of homes in the area you will be living in. This will give you a good idea, when you get there, of the simple square footage that your allowance will afford you. For instance, in some parts of the world, such as Hong Kong, Tokyo, and Singapore, in order to obtain decent-sized accommodation for a family of three to four people, your housing allowance may be more than your actual salary. Any less than US$5,000 per month in these cities will probably only get you a shoe box the size of the garage you left your tea chests in back home.
- Return airfares: Always insist that you and the entire family are entitled to at least one return airfare home each year, in business class if possible.
- Currency and exchange rate: Wherever your final destination may be, bear in mind that currencies can fluctuate wildly. Your employer will probably offer to pay you in local currency; however, if this currency weakens against your home country's currency you could find yourself, in the worst-case scenario, working for virtually nothing. Try to fix a rate with regular annual reviews. Or arrange to have your salary split into two parts, say, 50% paid into an offshore bank account and the other half paid to the country where you are working. For instance, when I first arrived in Singapore, I could get S$4.00 to one pound and I was paid in Singapore dollars. Consequently, paying off a mortgage at the rate of £2,000 per month cost me S$8,000 per month. Heavy stuff! Now of course it's approximately half that value and that particular mortgage is long gone, so I'm happy.
- Transport: Where possible try to arrange for you company to provide a car (and driver). In some cities where driving can be a nightmare, such as Bangkok or Jakarta,

this is essential. And make sure the running costs of the car, including gas and insurance, are also paid for.

- School fees allowance: There are many international schools with excellent facilities and curriculums, but they are not cheap. So, try to arrange that this is part of your package and do take the time to check out each school, which generally caters specifically to one nationality, i.e., American school, Australian school, and so on. Alternatively, if you prefer that your children continue their schooling at home, this will require some financial planning on your part (see Chapter 4: The school fees trap).

- Pension rights: gratuities and share options: As an expat, unless you are on a short-term assignment from your home country, you will not be allowed to continue to contribute to your home retirement scheme. This would include your 401K if you are from the United States, you superannuation if you are from Australia or your government pension scheme if you are from the U.K. So, during your period of absence from your homeland you will have a gap in your pension provision.

Therefore, you should also insist that some provision is made for this absence. In most cases, your employer will be an international player and may not have such a scheme available.

They may offer you a percentage of your gross salary as an additional increment to allow you to find your own alternative scheme. (This is covered in Chapter 9: The Pension trap).

They may even offer you share options in the company (take them as well). These incentives are not guaranteed to make you rich, as that will depend on how long you stay with the company and of course how well that company performs. If all else fails, ask what gratuities are available. These are normally paid to you annually or at the end of your overseas contract. The best contract will offer you a combination of all three options.

- Salary and bonuses: Always ask when your salary and bonus will be reviewed and have it put in writing.

- Trial period and termination of contract: Many expatriate contracts contain provision for a trial period in case the employee or the employer is not satisfied with the current arrangement. This is often followed by a pay rise to confirm the appointment (usually coinciding with the green light from Immigration on your employment pass or visa) or a pay-off if things don't work out. Be sure you understand and are happy with the terms of this arrangement and your redundancy package should your employment be terminated.

- Sickness and health benefits. Whether you are a single person or married with a family, always find out the terms and conditions of your (and you family's) sickness and healthcare benefits. These should cover everything from dental treatment to childbirth to emergency evacuation. So make sure that you are well covered and that the company pays for it, as private international healthcare insurance can be extremely expensive (see Chapter 5: The healthcare trap).

- Do your homework. If possible, try to arrange a visit to the country you intend to work in, just to make sure you and your family will be happy to live there. Also, check up on the details given to you by your employer or employment agency, or at least talk to someone who has worked there before.
- Club membership: Expatriates tend to work long hours, which often include a half day on Saturday as well. You no longer have the support network from family and close friends, so quality recreation time and a good social life are important. Making new friends overseas can be difficult. Don't forget that you're in a strange country and probably don't know many people apart from those you work with. You and your partner will quickly get bored with the poolside. A good idea is to negotiate a club membership, corporate if possible. Each nationality normally has various social clubs. However, the initial joining fees, annual subscriptions and monthly dues can be expensive. A family membership can cost from A$15,000 to AS$30,000 per year.

Put this proposal to the company you will be working for as well. It is the latest company perk that is well worth having.

- Seek professional advice: Lastly, before signing on the dotted line, engage a lawyer or employment consultant who specialises in overseas contracts to have a look at yours. You will have extra peace of mind knowing that all your (and your family's) needs have been met.

Arrival: the culture shock

Finally you arrive at your destination. You are placed in a hotel before finding accommodation to rent. It's hot, it's humid and the mosques are calling people to prayer over the loudspeakers every four hours. You are unfamiliar with the local customs and transport system. You quickly grow bored with hotel food and are wary of the local fare. If you are a non- working spouse you may feel lonely and isolated. Your immediate reaction may be 'What are we doing here?' You will be homesick and will miss the friends and relatives you waved off at the airport. However, looking forward, the company has now given you a housing allowance and you will have two to three weeks to find a flat or house of your choice. The children begin school, you make some new friends and start to settle into your new expatriate lifestyle.

Not so long ago I was sitting in a bar with one of my semiretired clients. Big John or BJ as he likes to be called, had just parked his yacht up in Singapore for a few days on his way down to Perth in Western Australia. Over a few drinks. BJ told me that money is no longer a worry for him at all. In fact, he was concerned about his golfing handicap in a forthcoming tournament in Perth, and that he had to replace one of his crew, as the standard of cuisine had dropped in the galley. I remarked, 'So life is tough, eh, BJ? Is there anything else bothering you at the moment? He Texan drawl said, 'Yeah…. I lost all my credit cards… Amex, gulped down another large Famous Grouse and in a deep Visa, Delt… All platinum…. All gone! Damn things!'

I asked if he had reported this to the usual card protection agencies and offered him my mobile phone there and then. He replied, 'No thanks, Mike. This happened awhile back…' And with a big grin on his face that looks just like John Wayne on a good day said, 'Hell, why would I want to replace them?' I just got a statement through and whoever's got my cards is spending a lot less than my wife did… So, I'm keeping quiet about this one, my friend!' The whole bar erupted with laughter and BJ ordered another round of drinks for everyone, and left laughing all the way to the lift.

So, you're moving up in the world…

Now you are an expatriate, enjoying what should normally be at least twice what you were earning before. Like many other expats before you, you will initially pay attention to paying off the credit cards, bills, and what's left of the mortgage. Then, as the saying goes, you only spend what you earn, right? Suddenly, you realise that your standard of living has risen dramatically. You may have a foreign maid or two. You will enjoy more meals out in nice restaurants. What used to be half-a-lager is now a gin and tonic. You spend the weekends lounging by the pool at your condo or playing golf or tennis at your private club. More expensive presents for everyone at Christmas and the Rolex watch you've had your eye onto straight onto your credit card. You may decide to join a wine club and fill your home with a selection of expensive wines. Not to mention the new Persian rug, antique furniture, designer clothes, the latest computer and hi-fi system and, of course, the bigger house back home.

profession is not of the same standard financially, think twice about purchasing such a large plot. They are costly to maintain if you have no other source of income to subsidise your reduced salary when you return home.

What's the point of owning a million-dollar property, knowing that when you repatriate your income may only be $75,000 to 100,000 dollars net after tax. On this amount, you may not be able to maintain a property like this, i.e., pay the bills, keep the place warm, pay a gardener, and so on…. The result would be an

But don't forget that the house on Bank Managers' Row will need to be maintained. And, like most expats, when you eventually return home, you will probably experience quite a large drop in income. In order to keep these nice new things, you will also need to maintain your larger income. However, this is not usually possible, as your income is likely to drop and your taxes will increase. So if your embarrassing sale to downgrade or renegotiate your expatriate contract and go back to the desert or the jungle, just to keep the big house and the wife happy. Remember, you made the choice to swap from "quality living" to a "higher standard of living".

A far better option, if you're into property, is to play the old monopoly game. It would make a lot more sense to invest in smaller, maintenance-free units or apartments that can be rented out and paid off slowly. There are numerous tax benefits from this kind of investing: namely, that the expenses can be negatively geared against your income. Then you would end up with an income from 5 to 10 apartments each month. Even after tax, this would pay the bills and fill the fridge in your home. Try to leave the big house till last. I have met some expats who are paying ridiculous sums of money just to keep up their large family homes while they are away. So forget about trying to keep up with the Joneses for the time being. It could end up setting you back and eating all the money you have worked so hard for. I will show you how to avoid this problem (and still have enough holiday money left over) in Chapter 14.

Most of us nomads go overseas for various reasons, whether it be the initial excitement of travel and the experience of different cultures, the food, the weather, and so on. We leave behind our upheaval of it all. Lt's face it, it can be hot and sticky, and it's a long way from civilisation as we know it. And because of the very transient nature of the expatriate lifestyle, it's often difficult to make friends and keep them. Ironically, we spend thousands of dollars every summer taking holidays in our own homelands.

So why does it? Well, simply because we like the money and the high standard of living it brings with it. Most expatriates I meet have a dream to save enough money to repatriate to their country of origin and live comfortably for the rest of their lives. However, only 3 in every 10 families ever save enough money to do so. Why? Because living an expatriate lifestyle is extremely expensive. Just think how much money you've spent in the past six months?

Overspending

Following on from the income trap, the asset trap basically means that you've gone and loaded yourself with the big house, the expensive car, beautiful furnishings, and the latest electronic gadgets which all eventually wear out or become outdated and need to be replaced. How many times have you been to a returned expat's home where the last time the place was redecorated was 10 years ago? Their hi-fi system will be well out of date, they still use a fax machine, and their car should belong in an auto museum.

So, what happens once you're living on a 'repatriated budget' and can't afford to maintain or replace your material assets?

The name of the game is not to live life as a frugal scrooge, but to concentrate on how to produce another source of income that will maintain your current lifestyle and allow you to replace the things that wear out. In other words, make sure that you have an independent income from an offshore source that will provide you with enough money to take care of you and your assets in later years.

With the obvious joy that comes with each new addition to the family, parents take on many responsibilities for their children's future. One of the most important is, of course, planning for their education.

From prep school to graduation: it could cost more than you think!

Some expatriate contracts will include provisions for your children to attend good international schools, wherever you may be stationed. However, these days many contracts are not that generous and more often than not the burden of school fees will rest with you. The better international schools do not come cheap. And even if the fees are paid for while you are away, this will stop if and when you repatriate. Not to mention the cost of tertiary studies later on.

At age 42, I already have two children of school age: Emma, 13 and Stephen 16, both at boarding schools in Australia. In order to provide my youngest son, Callum, aged 15 months, with the same standard of education, I will need to sit down and complete some simple mathematics to start saving for his school fees – now! Also, I have to take into consideration that by the time he reaches university age, I will already be 60 years of age. And I can assure you that I will not be wanting to pay for his tertiary education out of my own pocket at this stage in my life. For even at today's rates (of up to A $40.000 per annum for a good boy's senior boarding school) I will still have four or five years left to support him in his studies before he finds gainful employment: making me 65 years of age at this time!

With inflation running at a high 10% per annum,(at the time of writing this) these figures would be the equivalent of $68,000 per annum. Not good news for an upcoming pensioner like myself! I know I'm not on my own here, as many expatriates whom I've spoken to about school fees planning are in the same situation. Only last month, one of my friends repatriated to the UK, only to find that his teenage daughter, aged 18, had decided to become a surgeon. She had already been accepted by the Royal College of surgeons in Dublin, Which (at A$60,000 p.a.) required that he invest a lump sum of A$600.000 in order to endow the college with enough funds to see her through. Fortunately he was able to pay for this out of his Central Provident Fund pay out, so everything worked out well.

Start planning early

The secret to coping with your children's school fees is to start planning early. Once you have an accurate estimate of the total cost, you can set yourself a realistic payment schedule. My advice is this: start savings plan now based on your child's current age and school years left to complete. To get an accurate idea of the costs involved and for advice on choosing a school in Australia, you can visit a web site such as the Independent Schools Information service which is sponsored by the Australian (ATO). This site will bring you up to date with all the latest information about independent school in Australia, including a search facility for access to a school's prospectus and advice on academic success, admission and selection, day or boarding, fees, scholarships, and grants, and so on. It will also quickly bring you back down to earth! Especially all those people who thought they had this part of their financial lives covered.

You can also start a short – term savings plan, for a term say five years, or just for the term expected expatriate status. This can be achieved by investing a lump sum and a regular amount into an offshore savings plan with a financial institution of your choice. Trust me, after pondering over this duty – bound dilemma for many hours, I came to the conclusion that the only way to meet my obligations is to start saving and making my money work harder. This method ensures that your children receive the best education you can give. It also provides you with peace of mind, knowing you won't need to pay out large sums from your savings at the age of 55 or 60, when you may not have the means to afford it.

5 > THE HEALTHCARE TRAP

Security is a matter of choice. All healthcare glossaries will tell you something along the lines 'that being abroad can present you with all kinds of challenges. Standards of healthcare vary from country to country. Some parts of the world have a higher medical risk due to disease, suspect water supplies or public hygiene. Other areas have an adverse climate or inadequate safety precautions.....' The brochures also promise that you'll have peace of mind from knowing that you're well covered for all your medical needs – anywhere in the world, whether on holiday, at work or at home, whether it's for dental, optical or full-on heart surgery.

It pays to shop around

What they don't say up front is how much it costs. I recently made some inquiries with four of the leading healthcare companies in Australia, The premiums for comprehensive cover for a typical expatriate family of four: parents with two children aged 10 and 16 range from A$15,000 to A$ 25,500 per year.

If this is the kind of protection you are looking for, it pays to shop around. However, most expatriates already have some form of medical protection provided by their employer and they are also covered by basic government healthcare in their country of origin.

I have compared the above annual premiums with the cost of various operations one may be unfortunate enough to endure during one's lifetime, listed below in Singapore dollars. This is not to be confused with aged care or accidents, as these require a separate type of insurance.

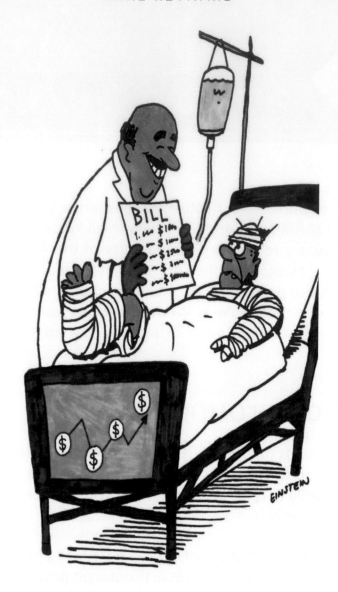

Procedure	Cost (A$)
Examination of lungs	400
Removal of Piles	1000
Hernia operation	1850
Removal of gall bladder	2500
Breast cancer operation	5000
Heart Surgery	7800
Kidney transplant	7500

You should also add the average cost of a stay in a Singapore hospital: S$2000 per day. Childbirth is covered only if you have held the policy for 12 months or more, so the cost of having one baby works out to be between S10,000 and S15,000 (approximately one year's premium).

In the 20 years I have been assisting expatriates (of all nationalities) with a multitude of personal financial requirements, only three have needed to use health cover.

Personally, I don't believe in it – and you don't get anything back after you stop paying.

Putting the money to better use

In my opinion, this money could be put to better use. If I invested the average premium from each of the four healthcare companies discussed earlier, of $4,500 (US$7,000) per year over a short term of five years, I could personally accumulate $45,000 to $50,000 (US$80,000). Enough for two triple heart by-passes and a new pair of lungs… and a holiday for the family to some people, but for your considerable investment, you don't get anything back.

6 > THE HOUSING TRAP

'What shall we do with the house?' is the question on many expatriates' lips. Do we rent it out? Do we leave it empty and employ a gardener? Do we leave the keys with the neighbours and ask them to keep an eye on it while we are away? Or do we simply sell up, move our things overseas and put the proceeds in a nice, safe bank or building society account?

Of course all the above options are personal choices which should be considered before your departure, or perhaps hallway through your overseas stint, when faced with the question: do we re-let or re-buy? A simple and economical solution is to rent out your home and let someone else pay the mortgage for a while. Eight out of 10 expats I meet normally rent out their properties while they are away.

This arrangement can work well, providing the rental income covers your monthly loan repayments and you have excellent tenants who look after your home. However, we have all heard the horror stories about the tenants from hell who don't pay their rent and wreck the house and garden. To protect yourself against this, you

need to organise an official rental agreement via a good local letting agent who will look after your interests. Most importantly, a letting agent will vigorously screen the rental applicants in order to find you the most suitable tenant. This kind of service will usually cost you an up-front letting fee of up to half the first month's rent, plus somewhere between 5% to 10% of your rental income each month. But it's well worth it. Remember, you will be far away and unable to deal with any problems when they arise.

Unless you are migrating and leaving your home country for good, it's always a good idea to retain a foothold in the local property market, as getting back in can be a very costly matter. (This is discussed in Chapter 11: The Inflation trap) Over the past20 years of booms and busts in the property market there have been more of the ups than the downs and unlike a bank account, you get capital appreciation as well as interest in the form of rent. With the former you only get interest and even when compounded at 5% or 6% per annum it still takes 12 years to double your cash.

Taxation on income derived from Australian property

Taxation derived from Australian property is an important factor that must be taken into consideration. As far as the (ATO) taxman is concerned, you can apply to the Inland Revenue for a certificate authorising your tenant or letting agent to make rental payments directly to you without deducting Australian tax. If in doubt contact the (ATO) at www.ato.gov.au This is an important basic rate must be withheld from all remittances of rent to you.

An important point to note is that most expatriate spouses do not work when overseas and therefore will always have a personal and marriage Australian tax allowance currently A$18.200. The personal allowance in 2023/24 tax year is also A$18.200 per annum and the marriage allowance was an additional A$1,260 per annum. The total allowance is $6,305 per year, a little over the $500 per month that could be claimed if the rental remittance was put in the spouse's name. She or he could then deduct the normal 10% per annum of the total rent collected as wear and tear. This works out to be a lot more cost effective that Mr Smith collecting the rental, as he will have no personal allowance if he is working overseas.

Example 1

John Smith earns $100,000 overseas and has no Australian personal allowance.

Income from rental per annum	12,000
10% deduction wear & tear	1,200
Net taxable income at 23%	10,800
Tax to pay on Australian property	2,484
Net Income	8,316

Example 2

Income from rental is put in John Smith's wife's name. Mary Smith has no income overseas as she doesn't work commercially. However, she does qualify for a personal allowance.

Income from rental per annum	12,000
10% deduction wear & tear	1200
Personal tax allowance	A$18200
Total allowance to be deducted	
Tax to pay on balance	nil
Net income	10, 800

So, by putting the rental income into Mary's hands and remitting it directly to her, the Smiths have saved A$10.800 per year. Naturally that taxman does not advertise this system, as it's not in his interest to do so.

Capital gains taxes on properties and other assets

There is no gains tax to pay on the disposal of your own dwelling whether you are resident or not. However, second and subsequent properties and other assets, when disposed of, are taxed. The exception is that after obtaining non-resident status (see Chapter 7: The tax trap), all profits made on all other assets outside your own property which are bought and sold during the years of your absence (i.e. non-Australian tax residence) will not be liable for capital gains tax in the Australia or the Commonwealth There is no rate of Australian CGT The net capital gain is included in a taxpayers assessable income and taxed along with their other assessable income at their marginal rate of tax. The top marginal rate of tax is effectively 47%, inclusive of the 2% Medicare levy. A chargeable gain that is realised each tax free (of non-chargeable event). Everything else over and above these amounts is added to that year's income which you have earned and is taxed at that rate – currently up to 47%. Plus 2% Medicare levy.

There are no tax benefits for married couples living in Australia

As mentioned earlier, husband and wife are each entitled to the annual exemption limit. This, is however only the A$18200 basic tax allowance before paying taxes. however, cannot be carried forward for future years. So, wherever possible, if you have returned to the Australia and still own assets with sizeable gains, try to fully utilise your joint annual capital gains allowance. Also, as a married couple living together, the transfer of assets between each other is indeed free of tax. Please note that this benefit of transferring gains or losses between spouses automatically ceases when a couple is permanently separated.

So, wherever possible, try to dispose of any additional assets while you are still overseas and preferably in the tax year prior to your repatriation. This will be covered in Chapter7: The tax trap.

Properties purchased via offshore holding companies

Those expats who wish to go full steam ahead and play monopoly for real (that is, retain their properties after they have repatriated) should consider setting up an offshore holding company. This can be purchased ready made with offshore company shareholders and directors who do not and have no intention of living in Australia. However, you must watch your 183 days per annum maximum length of stay in the Australia otherwise you will be deemed to be a resident again and would thereby lose all tax benefits. Offshore companies are not liable for withholding taxes made on gains disposed of in another or foreign country, and this currently stands at a world-wide rate of 15% (a lot less than 40%).

An offshore company will cost you between $1,000 to $2,000 and the same again every year as filing fees. You cannot sell or put an existing property you already hold onto an offshore company. It must be done the other way around.

Financing is arranged in a different way from an offshore bank. Deposits will be 40% to 50% of the purchase price, via a corporate loan system and, unlike your normal mortgage, the term of the mortgage is only 8 to 10 years and not the usual 20 to 25 years. So, the repayments will be a lot higher and so are the interest rates – usually 1% to 2% over those for a standard personal mortgage.

However, once underway, the full amount of interest paid i.e., 9% or 10% and of course the usual 10% wear and tear can be deducted on a loan back system from the 15% withholding taxes.

Once deducted from the 15% withholding tax that the company would be liable for on disposal of some or all its assets, the end result is a negligible tax bill.

I have known this system to be most favourable for the wealthier expatriate who can even go to Australia and lease or rent one of the properties on a long- term basis, and pay the rent straight back to the offshore company's bank account. All this is possible. Further information is available via our list of services.

7 > THE TAX TRAP

Adouble agreement basically means that if you have paid income tax in one country when working overseas, then you won't have to pay it again in your home country. This is not the case with the American taxation system; a unique system in itself that is not covered in this book. Instead, this chapter looks at Australia and Commonwealth system.

We all have to pay at some stage or another. These come under many guises, from income taxes to gains taxes to stealth taxes to name but a few. It is generally accepted that the more you pay in taxes, the more you put in your pocket. So, if the film stars and Pop stars of the world paid out 50 million dollars in taxes last year, they're not doing too badly.

Generally speaking, although you have less tax relief as an expatriate than you would have as a resident in your homeland, you most certainly have more opportunities to shelter your earnings from the taxman. This can be achieved via the many legal tax-free havens that still exist today using offshore banks, trusts, company bonds and a number of other vehicles which allow you to legally build up an anonymous tax-free nest egg. This can be accessed later using many different methods – from loan backs on lifetime trusts to the simple Gold Visa/debit card via the 20 million or so ATMs on most main streets' worldwide (see Chapter 14 for more details.)

Trust me, it works. As I write this book, while on vacation with my family on a small island in Greece, I have just been to the local ATM with my Gold Visa/debit card. Sure, Greek drachmas came out of the wall, but that's the local currency I need. And the hotel bill will be settled in a taxfree location where I still get interest on the money I've already spent, as it will take a couple of weeks at least to hit the Isle of Man for payment. Just think, 'virtual cash' that cannot be traced. It's great.

The rules: how the taxman sees us

Domicile

First of all, we all have our domicile to consider. This is the country or state that you consider to be your homeland. Your domicile is classed as separate from where you reside, or indeed your nationality. Whan you are born, in the eyes of the taxman although there are no death duties or inheritance estate taxes However, you may have tax obligations for the assets you inherit: capital gains tax may apply if you dispose of an asset inherited from a deceased estate. Income tax applies as usual to any dividends or rental income from shares or property you inherited.

However, if you are not happy with this arrangement you can abandon your original domicile if you decide to settle permanently in another country. You must, however, sever all links with your current or your father's domicile and move towards acquiring a domicile in the new country you have chosen to settle in. You must provide good evidence to the taxman that you wish to sever all ties with the old domicile. You can write to your local ATO tax office and ask for a domicile form, or, on line on the internet.

Residency

How do you prove to the taxman that you are a non- resident?

Basically, you must write to him first and explain your intentions – that is, that you are going to work overseas. If this is halfway through a tax year, then you may be able to have a tax rebate on the tax you have paid up until the day before you left (during the current tax year of your departure).

You will always be regarded as resident in Australia if you spend 183 days or more in one tax year there.

If you are in the Australia for less than 183 days, you will be treated as 'not ordinarily' resident. Were you to visit Australia regularly and, after four years, your visits during those years averaged 91 days or less in a tax year, from the fifth year onwards you will be treated as non-resident for tax purposes.

To claim as 'not ordinarily resident' you must aim to stay away for a full Australian tax year from beginning 1 July and ending30 June of the following year are generally due on the 31st of October after the end of the tax year.

For the rich and famous it is commonly known as the 90night to the many other places like the U.K. and may maintain their non – residency if they only spend 90 nights or less there. Before they leave Australia, ask the (ATO) tax office for details of this programme to be completed by individuals going abroad.

So, to recap, you may spend up to 183 days in a tax year in your homeland. However, this must not average more than 91 days in a tax year over four years.

Calculating annual average visits

The set formula that you can use to work out the average number of days spent in Australia each year is as follows:

Total visits to the AUS (in days) _____x 365 days = annual average visits

Total period since leaving (in days)

The maximum period over which the average is taken is four years.

For example, John Smith, a retired architect, left Australia on 23 November 2022. In the period from the date of his departure to 5 April 2022 he visited AUS for 43 days. In the following three tax years he spent 110, then 85 and another 57 days in AUS. The average number of days in AUS works out at 87.61 days.

43 + 110 + 85 + 57   295 x 365

The 183/day test is one of the tests used to determine if you are a resident of Australia for tax purposes
_____ = _365 + 87.61 133 + 366 + 365 + 365   1229 days

As this is less than 91 days per annum average, Mr Smith will be treated as non – resident for tax purposes throughout the four – year period.

So remember, 183 days or less or an average of 91 days per annum over four years in order to be treated as a non – resident throughout the period.

In my experience, most expatriates who have spent more than 6 to 10 years overseas never wish to return permanently anyway.

Many of my acquaintances return home for brief family gettogethers, weddings, and funerals only. I will explain how to avoid an unnecessary frosty welcome from the taxman in Chapter 13.

Stealth taxes

All governments tax us one way or another via indirect or stealth taxes. Governments are now imposing stealth taxes on products and essential services in every country around the world. Stealth taxes can be anything from GST, import duties, taxes on cigarettes, petrol, liquor, and so on (basically any indirect taxation other than income tax).

Such taxes compensate for a drastic miscalculation of revenue required for social security and pension benefits for their citizens.

Allan Greenspan (the US Federal Reserve Chairman) has publicly stated that the US government needs to inject at least US$700 billion into the stock market over the next 15 years, in order to aid or subsidise the country's retirement and sickness benefits. In other words, the coffers are almost empty.

We all know that these days people are living longer. So who is going to pay for the ageing population? The simple answer is you, via the snare of stealth taxes.

As honest citizens we all have a duty to pay income tax. For example, on a US$30,000 per annum income the average taxpayer will pay US$498,000 to the government in tax over his or her lifetime. This is more than he or she could hope to save. And this is at the lower end of the scale. If you are earning around US$100,000 a year you will pay in excess of US$2 million in lifetime taxes.

However, whatever you do with your tax-paid dollars (net income) is entirely up to you. This should be all yours to keep. Or is it? You can buy a house, a car, a boat or spend it as you wish, but those sensible types who want to save some cash for a rainy day or a nice retirement home overseas must pay tax on the savings again! How? In the form of tax on the interest accumulated in your bank account, or the profit earned from the sale of a property or shares, or capital gains taxes, or inheritance tax, to name but a few. But why should you? You are a responsible person who considers your and your family's future, you pay your taxes and you put something aside for that rainy day (possible retrenchment, school fees, a nice boat or a peaceful retirement in the South of France, and so on).

THE INHERITANCE TRAP

Death duties

Ninety percent of countries will tax their citizens by means of an additional tax called inheritance tax, commonly known as 'death duties.' This occurs upon the death of the person domiciled by origin of his original country.

Unlike some countries, in Australia there are no taxes on inheritances or deceased estates. A persons assets can pass directly to those they name in their legal Will without the involvement of taxation authorities.

In Australia, there are no inheritance tax or estate tax duties. However, you may have tax obligations for the assets you inherit capital gains tax may apply if you dispose of an asset inherited from a deceased estate. Income tax applies as usual to any dividends or rental income from shares of the property you inherited.

There are various methods of sheltering assets from the taxman on the transfer date of both parent's eventual demise, from wills to trusts and various exemptions like donations to charities, and so on.

This chapter primarily deals with inheritance tax and trusts, and some of the necessary steps that must be taken by international investors who are not currently resident in their country of origin. The following information contains a general outline in layman's language and is not intended to be taken as specific investment or taxation advice. Ideally, further advice is recommended relating to individual circumstances, on a case-by-case basis.

Potentially exempt transfers

The most significant feature of inheritance tax is the concept of potentially exempt transfers, such as:

- An outright gift to an individual
- A gift into an accumulation and maintenance settlement
- A gift into a settlement for the benefit of a disabled person
- A gift into an interest possession trust
- The termination of an interest in possession settlement where the sheltered property passes on to an individual as an accumulation and maintenance settlement, or a trust for the benefit of a disabled person.

The following exemption mainly concerns only those who are very rich (worth over US10 million. They may give away a portion or indeed all their wealth (including all their worldly goods and chattels) providing they live for at least 7 years after bestowing the gift, after which there is no tax payable on the amount handed over at all. The taxable amount payable scales down from 100% to nil at the $325,000 threshold. This however does not apply to Australians.

Time between gift and death	Percentage of tax payable
Not more than 3 years payable	100%
Between 3 and 4 years payable	80%
Between 4 and 5 years payable	60%
Between 5 and 6 years payable	40%
Between 6 and 7 years payable	20%
After 7 years	Nil payable

Gifts with reservations

A gift with reservations is treated differently from an outright gift, as it is a gift that you would like to continue to enjoy some benefit from after you have given it away. For instance, you may have an expensive oil painting but still hangs on your wall instead of in the house of the person you have given it to. Or' you decide to give away your large property, but instead of moving out, you still live in one of the rooms of the assets you have already given away.

In the taxman's this is treated as a gift with reservations and will be treated as yours until the date you cease to enjoy any benefit from it – or until the day you die. It will be taxed at the full amount. So, if you give your house to your children but still continue to live there rent free, your house would continue to be counted as part of your estate. The seven-year rule of tax exemption would not start until the day you either move out of the home or are seen to pay your children rent for the room you live in, even though the property is yours to begin with.

A sad but fact. Anyway, you would be far better off in the granny or granddad flat adjacent, paying a nominal commercial rent, all on the books and recorded by your accountant.

The only other exemptions are, as stated earlier, transfers between husband and wife during their lifetime and upon death.

Smaller gifts of up to $250 per annum may be given to anybody in the family without paying tax. Also, a marriage gift to your children of up to $3,000 can be given and is tax exempt.

Trusts

There are several ways of setting up trusts in order to shelter your lifetime gains from the taxman, using different kinds of trusts in various offshore jurisdictions.

Discretionary trusts

This is where income is distributed at the discretion of the trustees. The complex rules governing the practicalities of using offshore trusts to both minimise income tax and enhance tax-planning opportunities are numerous. However, if carefully planned, these can save you thousands (and millions – if you are in this category) even while you are still alive. For instance, take the current legal position of the large corporate life insurance companies who take it upon themselves to underwrite policies in the form of life bonds via lump investments. When these are written under trust while the settler (you) is still alive, the tax will fall on the settler. If the settler subsequently dies or if he or she is still alive and remains non- resident for tax purposes (that is, the settler has retired abroad) then the taxation will fall upon the trustees. If, however, those trustees are Australian residents, then the tax would be levied at 45% This can be totally avoided if, instead of choosing trustees who are Australian residents, you choose non-resident trustees. For example, the board of directors of an offshore life assurance company, with a household name and an excellent track record (of which there are many). Then the investor would continue to get gross rollup and the beneficiaries would only pay tax as and when they received the benefit, provided they are Australian residents at the time. If they too live overseas, think about the opportunities for lower or non-resident taxpayers. They would completely avoid having to pay the basic 34% tax.

Offshore insurance bonds

The practice of using offshore trusts via the purchase of an offshore insurance bond is not new and the practicalities of using a trust company format are straightforward and fairly simple. You would normally choose an intermediary (an expert offshore insurance or investment advisor) who is normally appointed as the fund or investment advisor) who is normally appointed as the fund manager. It is this person's job to help the investor to choose the correct portfolio weightings according to the individual client's wishes and their attitude towards risk or risk adversity. The advisor would then be the appointee and have full responsibility to switch between the range of funds available from the offshore insurance or investment company. The client can choose a cautious approach (deposit, fixed interest and government bonds) or a balanced or aggressive approach, or a combination of all three (as explained in Chapter 15: A model portfolio).

Lifetime insurance policies

The other simple method to settle death duty or tax bill is to take out a lifetime (whole of life) insurance policy, which is not taxed. On the date of the transfer or death of the settler, the proceeds of this policy are then used to offset the tax bill. I am not a big believer in this method of tax sheltering because, for a start, you have to be in very good health at the outset and the premiums increase as you get older.

9 > THE PENSION TRAP

Ask yourself how many jobs have you had so far in your career? If you've changed more than three or four times, think of all those frozen pension rights left behind in some old trust or on deposit. Do you even remember where they are or have any idea how they are performing? For most people the answer is no.

Most of us have indeed had several jobs with different companies during our careers. This means we have probably left behind various pension provisions in dribs and drabs all over the place. And when added together and put to one side, it's still not enough to retire on.

Why most people don't save

This is partly their fault and partly the fault of the financial services industry. The very word 'pension' makes most people cringe. Thoughts of old age and long-term financial commitment (with heavy early surrender penalties if premiums are stopped or the contract is cancelled before the end of the term) are things people avoid. And to make matters worse, there are commission-hungry salespeople in this industry who will sell you a savings plan for 10 years or more or a long-term pension (even to age 70+ if you let them.

A common mistake made by many expatriates is that they postpone indefinitely their pension arrangements. I've often heard people say, 'Ah well, I don't know how long I'll be here, so I'd best not commit myself to any sort of longterm financial arrangement...... I could be sent home any minute and that would be the end of that.' Yet I've met hundreds of expats over the years who have said the very same thing, and here they are 5 or 10 years later still living overseas. Maybe in another part of the world, but nevertheless they are still expatriates and they are still without a suitable pension or savings provision for their inevitable old age.

You might say, 'Well, if worst came to worst our government will pay us social security.' Well, I've got news for you. Government coffers worldwide are rapidly depleting due to the ageing population. More than twothirds of the world's population face poverty in retirement because they have not made adequate provision for a pension. And the picture is getting worse each year. Another true fact: in most Western countries, within approximately 15 years there will only be one person working to support three retire people.

Or you may be thinking, 'Well, we won't need as much when we retire. The kids have gone and we don't have a mortgage anymore,' Think again. Inflation, above all, will erode your savings. For example, $100,000 at a meagre 5% inflation will only be worth half its value or $59,000 in 10 years from now. And I haven't even covered sickness.

Ageism hits pensioners hard

There was a time when two-thirds of your final year's salary would be adequate as a pension, but that's when people only lived to age 75 and not to 95+ as we do today. I'm not a demographic scientist, but I often wonder how people will be able to sustain themselves for what could be up to 30 to 40 years of retirement on the amount they managed to save during the previous 30 to 40 years (or half their lives). An impossible feat!

People are living a lot longer than ever before. With the assistance of medical science, those people fortunate enough will be able to buy body parts and continue living for another 10 to 20 years. So, unless you want a job as a part-time cleaner or behind the counter at the local McDonald's, take heed and put some money aside into your own personal offshore pension plan.

This is an investment opportunity available exclusively to expatriates, so save your cash while you are in the fortunate position to earning well. The shock of sudden repatriation for those ill-prepared could mean financial ruin or, at the very least, financial discomfort for those who still. have large mortgages and other outstanding debts.

An ideal retirement plan

So, what exactly is a good pension? Well, standard corporate practice is that a pension should equal twothirds of your final salary and be enhanced with annual increases that cushion against inflation. Yet only 16% of men and 14% of women actually reach this goal. And even the very best of corporate pension schemes can result in a drop in living standards.

The model retirement package of today may not always be the ideal scheme of tomorrow. Just as you will move on towards an active retirement your money will also require active management.

Three things you can be sure of: you will get old, you will need a retirement income and that income must increase each year, in order to take care of inflation.

So, what's the answer? There are four options available to you:

- Don't bother doing anything and risk being poor and sick in your old age. You can always sell the house and move into a bedsit or old people's home.
- Win the lottery – and there's a 10 million to one chance of this happening!
- Save it. Save it. And live frugally for the rest of your life.
- Save it and invest it wisely in an offshore pension plan. Your goal here is to accumulate enough capital to protect yourself with a tax-free income for your retirement, while maintaining the standard of your current lifestyle.

Offshore portable pensions

Why an offshore pension? Well, there are a whole host of reasons. Firstly, it earns gross interest and is out of reach of the taxman. It is totally private and anonymous. It is also completely portable and will travel with you regardless of any changes in your employment. In addition, it can be invested in offshore mutual funds and unit trusts where you will have access to the world's leading fund managers. Lastly, you can cash it in well before your 65th birthday, which you cannot do with onshore pensions (and so enough governments going to have to increase the pensionable age to 70 or even 75).

You can arrange the proceeds to be paid into any offshore or Swiss bank account (of your choice) gross of any tax deducted at source. Surely that makes sense. So don't waste this unique opportunity to attain financial security. Take full advantage of your privileged status as an expatriate and save as much as you can during the years you are in this position. Then reduce the premium when you repatriate and continue to feed it from an offshore account. This way your nest egg remains healthy and completely anonymous.

Withdrawals can be taken in lump sums or as regular income each month, paid into your offshore bank account. All you have to do is ramble down to the local ATM and draw down the amount of cash you require, in your local currency. It's as simple as that! Or pay for goods on line.

As one client recently commented, 'You know Mike, after all these years of paying off mortgages, school fees and many other Peter Pan… it's high time I did something for myself and make sure I have a stress-free retirement. So give me one of those offshore plans.'

How much should you save?

The amount you should save will depend on:

- How old you are now, i.e., how many years you've got left to go.
- Any other (if any) provisions you have already made.
- The standard of living you wish to maintain. Between10% to 25% of your net monthly wage normally suffices.

If you're still unsure how much to save, you can also use the following equation as a rough guide: Divide your age by two and use this figure as a percentage of the salary (take-home pay) you should be saving. For example, a person aged 40 (divided by 2 = 20) should be saving 20% of their net salary. Lump sums can be added and contributions can be increased at any time. And you don't have to wait till you're 60 to 65 to draw it down. If you can relate this exercise to my advice on tax-free savings (see Chapter 14), you should never experience a fall in living standard or pay unnecessary taxes on your offshore pension.

As president of 'Island Watch,' the local resident brokers association, my part-time vocation is to keep the expatriate financial services industry in Singapore clean. We aim to deter unscrupulous foreign salespeople from making raiding trips to Singapore. These commission sharks will try to sell people unnecessary and unsuitable products, with little

or no follow – service. This ultimately gives the entire industry a bad name, so it's in or interest to try to slow them down by educating the public. With the assistance of the strict operating laws enforced by the Monetary Authority of Singapore, so far, we have been winning the battle. However, over the years I have heard all sorts of complaints from people who are unhappy with the investments they have been sold. These people have been cold called by salespeople who usually will not disclose where they got their name and phone number – most probably from an embassy list or even the phone book. Western names do stand out! They will try to sell you everything from long-term insurance policies, real estate in some obscure country, stocks and shares, diamonds from Amsterdam, promising 200% growth in five years!

If you receive any cold calls at home or at the office from these sharks, a good tip is to politely ask the person where they obtained your name and whether this is a cold call. If they start to waffle on or finally admit that it is a cold call – then simply cut it short. You can be sure they won't call you again. As I don't know one end of an ostrich from the other, I can't help you there. But I can tell you that every industry has its fair share of crooks. So beware whom you invite into your office or your home. And watch out for those sharks!

Choosing a sound financial adviser is clearly of paramount importance, so it pays to spend some time shopping around before committing your hard-earned cash to any one arrangement.

Here are a few pointers to help guide you when choosing an investment adviser:

- Watch out for the visiting broker who sells only long-term investment plans (10 years or more). This is done in order to make enough commission to cover travel and accommodation costs. The longer the term of the plan the more commission that is paid out.
- Avoid the 'day-tripper' or 'raider' with a return air ticket to KL or London in his back pocket. You can spot visiting brokers by the obscure overseas address on their business cards. Instead, find a local adviser whom you can contact 24hrs a day and will attend to your queries immediately.
- Ask about the broker's track record -not only of the funds they are invested in, but also of 'live' accounts that they manage. Ask to see current statements of their clients' investments, which will indicate their fund allocation, performance, and growth since the commencement of the investment.
- Do not pay any money direct to the broker, only to the financial institution you are investing with.
- Always ask if the broker has access to a fund switching facility, whereby you can arrange fir either you or your broker to have chosen to invest with. This way you are not stuck in non- performing funds, when in fact your investment allocation range of funds offered. Without this arrangement, your investment could have devalued significantly by the time you see your broker again.

- Never pay up-front fees on your investment or hefty fees for fund switching. And beware of 'churning.' This is where brokers make commission every time they buy and sell on a regular basis.
- After reading the brochure, always ask for a copy of the terms and conditions of your investment before signing on the dotted line.
- Avoid paying early and unnecessary surrender penalties.
- Avoid over committing yourself: a 5-year investment should suffice for most expatriates. Like many expats, you may only be working overseas for two to five years, during which time your circumstances could change very quickly Certainly, your lifestyle and income are significantly altered once you repatriate.
- Ask for some references or testimonials from existing clients.
- Ask the broker what sort of regular feedback or after-sales service they provide: monthly newsletters, yearly performance reports, regular up-to-date statements, and so on.
- Beware of financial advisors who fail to ask you about your short and long-term goals and specific financial requirements.
- Don't be afraid to ask the broker about the commission they make on the products recommended to you.
- Don't feel pressured to invest immediately with the first proposal you are shown. Take your time to shop around and make your own comparisons of other products or services on offer.
- If in any doubt the credibility of the broker, the products, or the company they represent, run the proposal by an independent third party, such as your accountant or lawyer, or the MAS (Monetary Authority of Singapore). You can also ask your potential broker which licence they hold. One of the most stringent is the IMRO licence issued by the Isle of Man regulatory Authority. Or inquire whether the company they represent has been given the green light to operate in Singapore by the Commercial Affairs Department.

Remuneration

Of course, a good financial advisor should be paid some kind of financial recompense for their hard work, which usually will involve research, advice, administration and fund management. This is best arranged on a performance-related basis, ideally in arrears (after you are satisfied with the performance of your investment). For example, 1% of the total funds under management, paid annually in arrears, based on a minimum net growth of 10% percent per annum. Anything below this amount is unacceptable and I would advise you to find yourself another advisor!

Public enemy number one

e verything else but inflation. Governments hate it. House buyers are terrified of it. Pensioners dread it and housewives deplore it. So, what <u>about us poor expatriates? We go abroad, work twelve</u> hours a day, save like mad, then when it comes time to go home the price tag on that dream house has gone up so much it's virtually out of reach… And to make matters worse, you can remember exactly how much it cost when you left.

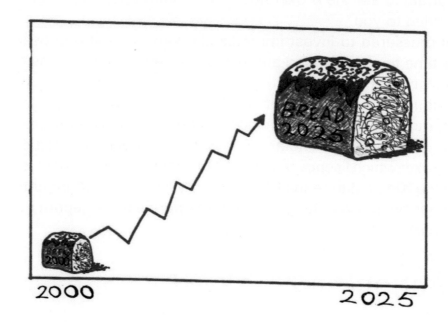

I won't go into all our yesterdays, but just recently I returned to Australia after an absence of only two years. I found that a pack of cigarettes had gone up to $14.17 for ultra mild, when the same pack cost only $4.50 two years ago. Even more disturbing, a pint of beer was nearly $16.00 in London. What on earth will I have to pay for a pint when I retire in 15 years', I wonder?

The model system

Look at Switzerland for example. It's a fact that this country never endured the hardship or legacies of the first and Second world wars. It did not need to borrow money from overseas countries and have to pay millions of dollars in interest each month in war loans (the UK is still paying millions of pounds to the US for loans during WW11). Nor has it ever had to rebuild any of its cities. Switzerland has always been a place where people put their money when all other countries were at war. Its environment is safe and clean. It has very little inflation and its interest rates have always been approximately 1% per annum.

This makes the Swiss Franc one of the strongest currencies in the world. In an ideal world, every nation would like to model itself on Switzerland.

On the opposite side of the coin, a poor country like Chile, for example, has interest rates as high as 25% and inflation even higher at 45% to 50% and rising every month. Even the peasants take their wages home in a wheel-barrow.

I have vivid memories of my early years as an expatriate offering financial advice to people in Singapore. This was in the early 80s when the expats I was advising were about my age now (60+). They will be 65 + now and enjoying their retirement, having left Singapore after doing their 25 years. I was told of how they used to be able to get $8.00 or $9.00 Singapore dollars to the pound... back in the days when you could walk from Raffles Hotel across Beach Road and actually be on the beach.

Land reclamation had just begun and the old Bugis Street was still jumping with life. Anyone who was there at that time can tell you that things were very different. I myself arrived at the tail end of it and thoroughly enjoyed it.

Back to the jungle

John Smith, a good friend and client, was aged 55 at that time in 2017. An architect, He decided to call it a day and go back to bonny Scotland to retire and play golf (his favourite pastime). John's children had grown up and moved on. He also had a decent pension of $60,000 per year and $450,000 pounds saved in the bank. We said our goodbyes. Afterwards I used to visit him and his family on the occasional Scottish summer trip or Hogmanay. However, within 3 to 4 years John was back in Singapore. I was surprised to see him and asked what in the world he was doing back there. He replied, 'I need the work, Mike.... $2500 a month will nae pay the way.'

I have since met well over a hundred John Smith's. Hardworking, likeable guys who make every effort to make things secure financially for themselves and their families. However, like John by not calculating how this would affect their retirement or repatriation. As a result, the only answer was forget about retirement and go back to the jungle.

12 > THE TOO LONG OVERSEAS TRAP

One piece of advice I find myself repeating to new arrivals is: beware of over-extending your financial commitments – or you might end up having to extend your contract and stay longer than you think.

The strain on the marriage

I have met some expatriates who, for one reason or another, sadly cannot afford to repatriate. You may relate to this situation (as explained in earlier chapters dealing with assets, income and inflation) when reading this brief but true account. The expatriates who fall into this trap have unwittingly made a noose for their own neck by overextending their financial commitments back home. Often, their families have already returned home to resume normal life. However, the outgoings are such as summer holidays and the occasional Christmas. They have either fallen for the asset trap or the income trap (or both) and are probably sending their children to the best schools or universities. Sadly, because of the obvious strain on the marriage, after a number of years, long term separations do not make the heart grow fonder – in fact quite the opposite, couples tend to grow apart. More often than not, this kind of arrangement ultimately ends in divorce.

Then, after many years of living away and having sacrificed family number one, it becomes increasingly difficult to return home and pick up where you left off. It's a kind of culture shock in reverse. Finally, it becomes easier to just to continue living overseas and a lonely long-term male expat will often seal his fate by marrying a local wife. His new wife, like her Western counterpart, rarely concedes to live abroad for long. So even if he manages to talk her into returning home with him, her strong desire to go back to her home country and family usually brings them back to where they started. These men usually end up becoming permanent or terminal expatriates. They come from all walks of life: from CEOs of international banks, accountants, lawyers to schoolteachers and oil engineers (not necessarily in that order).

I have not met many Western retired couples in Singapore or south-East Asia. The Far East is usually a place to work and live comfortably while you have a work contract.

This is a very touchy subject which every expat family has to consider. I have tried many combinations of solutions myself. During the early years of my first marriage, my children lived with me in Singapore until the ages of 3 and 3. Then it was time for school and after seven years in Singapore, my wife decided she had had enough. So, we decided to send the whole family back to the UK (that was in the mid-1980s). Initially things went well. I spent one month away and then one month at home. Then came the bigger house and all the other trappings, so the overseas trips were extended in order to cover the rise in living standards and support a growing family. It then became two months away, one month at home, then three months away, one month at home, and so on….

The end result: we simply grew apart. You can't see your wife three times a year when she's only 30 years old and you're 32, and reasonably expect to stay married. In any case, my job is to look after expatriates and you don't find many expats on the high street in Nether Wallop

Hertfordshire: they tend to live and work overseas.

Well, that was a long time ago and the family has come through it and is well taken care of. Now I divide my time between Melbourne and Singapore (on a much briefer turn-around time) with my new wife and young son. I also spend no more than three or four weeks away from my family. This system can mean a drop in income but hour for hour you actually get more quality time with your family than a full-time man at home, who arrives home from the office at 7 or 8 pm, has dinner and goes to bed – and only sees the kids briefly at breakfast or on weekends.

If you are in the fortunate position of having an occupation that has an office in the same organisation or industry back home, then you are lucky, as the door is always open for you to return home. There is no easy solution. However, after interviewing thousands of couples, I have found that the most successful way of keeping your marriage together is to sit down together and agree on a time scale for your expatriate adventure. Then stick to it, whether it's three years, five years, or ten years (at the very most, or you will find it very hard to return home). Always keep this time frame in mind and plan for your financial security to ensure that when that time comes you are ready and able to leave. This is the only system that works; otherwise, you may find yourself moving back and forward, which in itself can be financially and emotionally draining.

'll keep this chapter short and sweet. It's always sad to say goodbye to all the friends and colleagues you have made during your first (and perhaps not your last) posting overseas. I myself headed home after 10 years. Then, after only one year back in the UK, I decided to come back to Singapore. In my experience, the longer you stay away the harder it is to settle back into your old lifestyle. For this reason, I often refer to this island as 'Hotel Singapore' – you can check out any time you like, but you can never leave.

A vicious cycle

Over the years I have seen many expatriates, particularly those who were here for some time, return to Singapore for various reasons – usually financial. Many people's primary aim in working overseas is to pay off large mortgages. However, few actually realise the opportunity to live in these homes. Once repatriated, they simply can't afford to run the 'big house' on lower wages. And if they are retrenched and have no other source of income, they are well and truly in the mire. The end result is a downgrade to a more modest abode. A sad but true fact, and a common story I've heard from many returning expatriates who've had to resume working abroad just to continue paying the bills at home. A vicious cycle, indeed!

So, it's finally time for you to go home. You've done your stint, paid off the mortgage and maybe even bought another property or two. On top of this, if you have been sensible, you will have also accumulated enough cash in the bank to make sure your impending arrival has a soft landing. And if you've planned your repatriation correctly, the only thing you'll have to worry about is where to place the ginger jars and hand-woven rugs.

Repatriation and taxation

Always expect the unexpected. Depending on what 'tax' time of the year you head home, don't be surprised if you received a frosty reception from the taxman. In his eyes, there are some basic guidelines that each returning resident should take into consideration well before booking your flight home. A general pointer is to try to arrange your financial affairs in the tax year prior to the year of your return home. If, however, you have been overseas for at least five whole complete tax years or more, you will have achieved the grand status of being 'non-resident' for all tax purposes. This means you will not be liable for any taxes on gains made on the sale of a second or subsequent property purchased, or any taxes payable on the sale of any shares, stocks or bonds, providing they are sold prior to your repatriation.

If you have been abroad for less than three years, then you will be classed as 'not ordinarily resident.' Ideally, your affairs should be put in order in the tax year prior to the year of your return. Otherwise, you may be liable for gains and interest earned from all assts, in the tax year you regain your residency.

Remember, from the day you arrive home you will be classed as a 'resident' again for tax purposes. This will include income tax at whatever rate your government decides to levy upon you. As you know, this can be anywhere between 25% and 65% depending on your country of residence. The taxman would like you to repatriate your cash and will encourage you to do so. This will include closing down or selling any offshore assets, so he has a better chance of taxing them. You are also obliged to declare all your worldly assets and any income generated from these assets, as well as any interest earned in any overseas bank accounts.

Minimising your tax bill

A simple method to minimise your tax is to close your offshore accounts, preferably in the tax year prior to your return. For example, if your tax year begins in April, try to close the account in March in the year prior to your return, otherwise you could be liable to pay tax on all interest earned in that year, even though you were living overseas.

If you hold any offshore mutual funds, trusts or similar investments that show large gains but are not linked to a life assurance policy (and you are forced to repatriate in the middle of a tax year) you can arrange to 'bed & breakfast' your funds. This means that you instruct your fund manager to sell your holdings in order to realise any gains made while you are still 'non-resident,' and simply buy them back, if you wish. This minimising any gains made before you re-join your home tax system and can be transacted as late as one month before you return home.

What the taxman doesn't advertise…

One of the major financial benefits of the expatriate contract) on top of the lucrative salary and bills footed by the company) are the existing legal loopholes available exclusively to expatriates. These can be a powerful tool when it comes to paying your tax bill and, when manged properly, can help cut your tax bill on investment income by half.

Overseas investment income and stealth banking

Generally speaking, all income from investments abroad, after you have repatriated, are considered taxable in the taxman's eyes. This could be income from interest earned in offshore deposit accounts, dividends paid on offshore shares, rental income from offshore properties and basically anything that produces an income. If and when these funds are remitted home or accumulated offshore, as an honest citizen who has repatriated, you are duty bound to declare this income annually on your county's tax self-assessment form. You must inform the tax department of how much money you have earned, where those assets are and how much you have drawn down as an income or gain from its source, where ever that may be.

These days, however, due to the ever-decreasing lack of paperwork, the trail to the tax man is being almost entirely eliminated. For instance, most offshore banks offer as standard the following services.

- A hold-mail service, whereby no mail is sent to your onshore address
- No more cheque books or paying-in books are required for either single or multi-currency accounts
- Complimentary Gold Visa/debit card: Normally, most of the offshore banks will offer you the above services plus a complimentary Gold Visa/debit card. This has replaced the cheque book and your account can be accessed via any of the 20 million ATMs around the world as the amount drawn down is automatically debited from your offshore account. For further details, refer to the section on tax effective savings in Chapter 14. Nowadays people use online banking services.

For the movement of larger amounts of money, most offshore banks will also include the additional services of online banking or telephone or facsimile instructions. The bank will ask you to nominate a password that works the same way as a PIN number when you use your debit card via an ATM. Online banking services are now available via the telephone or internet banking 24 hours a day, 365 days a year, so computer literate clients can check the balance of their accounts and move money from point A to point B quickly and easily. All of this is designed to simplify banking, whilst reducing the paper trail to the taxman – and it works.

A bank account of course, will not make you rich, and is only there as a handy tool for paying bills, taking cash from the hole in the wall, moving money around and convenience while travelling.

Offshore investment bonds (lump sum investments)

One of the most tax effective methods of sheltering your cash from any of the taxes mentioned above is to purchase an offshore bond from a life assurance company – before you repatriate. The bond is held by the life assurance company in your name. This investment vehicle has access to all the world's major financial markets and fund managers, most of which are household names with excellent reputations and solid track records. Fidelity, Invesco,HSBC Henderson, Jardine Fleming, ING Barings, Gartmore, HSBC, Lazards, Newton, Perpetual… to name but a few. You can invest in fixed interest currency investments, similar to a bank account, and mutual or equity funds. If you are risk adverse, you can even choose a cautious approach with any of the above – mentioned fund managers. Most of these companies do not charge any up-front loading charges or fund-switching fees, so you are on to a winner by having all of your money go to work for you immediately.

These days there is no up-front loading on the initial investment, so your money goes to work immediately. You also have the option to draw down an income from your lump sum immediately. The mode of payment can be monthly, quarterly or annually directly paid into a bank account of your choice, anywhere in the world. Income payments are paid gross of any tax deducted at source. This is achievable because you are a non – resident of the jurisdiction where your money is invested.

More importantly, an offshore investment bond will allow you to automatically qualify for two types of powerful personal tax relief.

Personal tax relief after repatriation

Time apportionment relief

This is a very generous tax relief recognised and granted by most governments. It works insofar as it allows you to keep your investment bonds offshore long after you have repatriated, rather than the reverse and en-cash them unnecessarily just because you have to go home.

The relief works by reducing the chargeable gain by any time spent outside your country of residence during the term of the investment with the life assurance company. For example, if you have held an investment bond for five years and three of those years were spent overseas, then two-thirds of the gain automatically qualifies for time apportionment relief and will not be liable for gains tax. This is granted by the taxman because of a simple legal loophole. It stipulates that whoever holds an offshore investment with an offshore life assurance company should hold the minimum of 1% of the value of their initial investment as a life assurance contract. This makes the investment bond look like a life assurance policy, even though the life assurance content (at 1%) is very minimal.

For example, if Person A invested $100K, the life office would issue the investor 1% of the initial investment, this being only31,000 (the minimum amount required by the taxman). And if the investment was US$1 million, the life assurance content of the plan would be equal to only US$10,000. You can see why many millionaires prefer this style of investment.

5% annual income withdrawal allowance

The other source of tax relief allowed to Australia and Commonwealth investors is called the 5% Annual income Withdrawal Relief, whereby the taxman will defer any chargeable gains drawn down as income from an offshore life assurance bond until after your repatriation. This form of relief is effective from the day you start your investment bond (while you are 'non-resident') thus giving you an accumulated 5% per annum of the original value of your bond 0for each year you have held on to it. For example, retaining your investment bond offshore for say, three years prior to repatriation would automatically qualify you for a tax-free draw down of 15% of the value of your bond as tax free income, even though you are a taxpayer back home. Any unused 5% per annum is rolled up for future years, i.e., 5yrs = 25%, etc… a lucrative annual windfall.

Typically, many expatriates withdraw a monthly, quarterly, or annual income from their offshore bonds (on average 10% per annum, which is not uncommon.

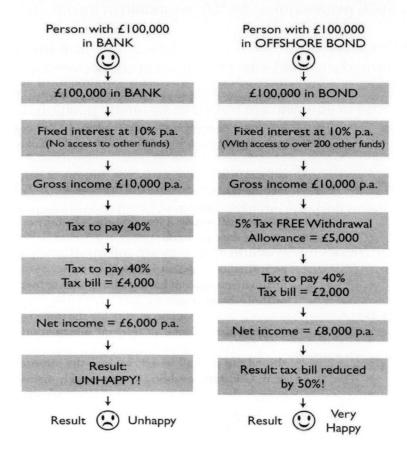

To understand how this form of tax relief works please refer to the chart which demonstrates the definite advantage of holding money in an offshore bond as compared to an offshore bank account, using the 5% income withdrawal allowance. I will be generous and say the interest from the bank account is 10% per annum and grant the same growth rate for the investment bond.

This simple chart clearly shows how to legally reduce your investment income tax bill by half. And do keep in mind that, unlike the simple bank term deposit, the life office has on average a range of over 200 investment funds to choose from. Offshore bonds also have a high potential investment performance compared to their onshore counterparts, which are heavily taxed.

The above illustrations are based on exactly the same interest rates and have not taken into consideration time apportionment relief (any gains made in an offshore insurance bond while you were non-resident are not taxed at all). And as a non-resident of the isle of Man, you as an investor, will not be liable for any withholding taxes, death duties or income taxes. Everything is paid to you gross and nothing is deducted at source. So, it's not hard to imagine why people with large sums to invest (or multiples thereof) can see the many advantages of starting an offshore investment bond now. In my experience, most expatriates draw down approximately 10% of their offshore investments to maintain their current lifestyles and take care of inflation. By using this system, someone with $1 million in an investment bond who draws down 10% per annum or $8,333 per month will automatically save $50K per annum or $4,150 per month in income tax.

Although past performance is no guide to the future, offshore investment bonds have consistently outperformed any fixed-interest deposit account over any 5 – year period since the Second World War. And there's no reason to suggest any change in performance in years to come. For those of you who are not in the fortunate position of having a lump sum to invest, there are similar offshore investments to which you can contribute on a regular monthly basis, that also qualify for the same tax relief.

For Australian residents, all relevant information relating to various tax relief self-assessment forms and guides to living and retiring abroad can now all be accessed via the internet and easily read in A, B, C format, enabling you to quickly assess your own position as far as the taxman is concerned. The web site is and the relevant information booklets and forms to look at and print off are as follows:

The repatriation trap

IR 20 Residents and non-residents – liability to tax in Australia should contact the Australian tax office Direct www.ato.gov.au

Do take advantage of this helpful information for any of the above situations, from letting your home to retiring abroad. The taxman has prepared this information especially for expatrites so don't hesitate to use it as a reference.

14 > SOLUTIONS – SOME HANDY INVESTMENT TIPS

ow we have established why we are here. We have identified the pitfalls and the bonuses of expatriate life and know what we want to do. So, how are we going to achieve it?

SOLUTION: The simple answer is SAVE IT OFFSHORE TAXFREE!

Make the most of your expatriate status: use it or lose it!

Your current overseas address holds the key to your financial success. As an expatriate, you have a window of opportunity to invest monies overseas into tax-free jurisdictions, such as Isle of Man, Jersey, Guernsey, each of which is sworn to secrecy about its depositors. However, once you become a resident again, that's it, the doors are closed. In a nutshell, it means that all offshore banks and financial institutions in these time-honoured jurisdictions insist that:

- You are non-resident of your country of origin.
- You have an overseas address.
  So don't leave it too late!

Tax-effective savings: the benefits of banking in an offshore environment

So, what does the term 'offshore' mean exactly? To some this may conjure up a picture of a tiny island somewhere in the Bahamas, which in turn may prompt you to think 'Oh, that's too far away!'

But the questions most people want answered is, 'Is my money safe?', followed by, 'Is it accessible when I need it?' the first and most important step in building an offshore nest egg is to choose a safe haven or jurisdiction in which to place it.

For my money, I have found the isle of Man to be a safe and reliable offshore centre for over 20 years. For those of you who are unsure exactly where this is, the Isle of Man occupies a central position in the Irish Sea, as well as the British Isles. The island itself is some 33 miles 952 km) long from north to south and 13 miles (22km0 wide from east to west. This makes it only a little larger than Singapore, although the population is only just over 70,000. Dating back to Viking origins over one thousand years ago, the Isle of Man Tynwald government claims to be the oldest legislature in the world in continuous existence. As a government in its own right, the Isle of Man only looks to the UK for armed protection (and pays an annual fee for this service). The island is also very proud of its coat of arms, which features the three legs of man and the Latin "Quicunques Jerceris Stabit", meaning "Whichever way you throw me, I stand."

The distinguishing feature of offshore banking is that it allows you to keep your money safely tucked away from the prying eyes of the tax man. After all, you've paid some kind of tax on it once already (as discussed in Chapter 7), so why pay tax on it again and again?

The main reason why the Isle of Man is clearly one of the safest offshore havens is that unlike any other jurisdiction in the world, it has a depositor's protection scheme guaranteed by the government. Should a bank or financial institution ever become unable to meet its abilities, your money is guaranteed up to 90% with no upper limit – all backed up by the Isle of Man government and its strict Financial Supervision Commission. Investor protection is what the island's reputation is based on. In addition, it has installed an arsenal of money laundering measures and is not on the non – compliance hit list by G7 and the OECD (the anti-money laundering organisation that has been investigating currency crime in offshore jurisdictions since 1989). The FATF recently issued a list of non- co-operative regimes, but neither the isle of Man or the Channel islands were on that list.

Even the US inland Revenues gave the Isle of Man its vote of confidence, saying that it had complied with the Us withholding tax legislation. Unlike some of the lesserknown tax havens, the Isle of Man compels foreign financial institutions to implement stringent "know your customer" regulations in order to discourage money laundering and tax evasion.

However, no declarations are made to any governmental authority about its investors (no matter which government asks the questions or who the depositor is). And all the major international banks are represented with offshore branches. The Isle of Man alone has up to 60 major banks and financial institutions to choose from.

Another important feature of offshore online banking is that interest rates (which are paid gross) are very competitive and investors currency of their choice. For example, using my Visa/debit card from my offshore bank account, I can access my cash 24 hours a day, 365 days a year via any of the 20 million ATM, Visa or delta machines around the world. And with telephone, facsimile and now internet instructions, I don't need a cheque book or regular statement to leave a tell-tale paper trace to the taxman. I also don't pay any annual subscription fees for my Visa Card and all my standing orders are free. And I don't have to stick to only one currency. Through my multi-currency account I have a choice of eleven major hard currencies. When travelling through Europe, I can use my EURO Visa card to pay for hotel bills, cat rental and so on, and all bills are subsequently settled via my bank account in the Isle of Man. This means I can earn interest on the funds in my Isle of Man account for up to five weeks after I've spent the money. The idea is that you shouldn't have to pay for converting currencies. And you don't have to be a millionaire to open an offshore account. Most deposit accounts can be opened with a minimum deposit of $2,500 or US45,000 (S$6,800) including card facilities.

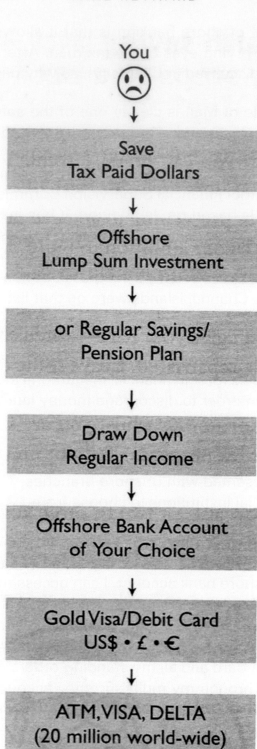

Stealth saving with invisible cash: eight easy steps to a tax-free anonymous nest egg

So now you can practise some 'stealth saving' of your own with your offshore invisible cash! Follow the eight easy steps in the diagram preceding to achieve tax-effective offshore savings:

If it's your ambition to build up tax-free, anonymous nest egg during your stint as an expatriate and pay a lot less tax when you go home, try to keep the following advice in mind:

- Don't give your hard-earned cash to your government after you have repatriated. Leave some of it working offshore!
- Investigate the possibilities of offshore banking and investment opportunities whilst you are still an expatriate or non-resident (for tax purposes0/ and not on the way to Changi Airport as you leave.
- Allow at least two to three years to build up your offshore tax-free nest egg, not two to three months.

- Remember, you need an overseas address to open an account. Once you have qualified and set up your investments you can update your address or change it to a hold-mail service or PO Box at a later date
- After you repatriate your tax-free, anonymous nest egg remains working for you overseas, and not the other way around for a change.
- As the taxman will not know where you bank offshore, it's difficult for him to tax 'invisible cash' with no statement or cheque books, only telephone or facsimile instructions from yourself and access to your cash via your Vis/debit cards, from virtually anywhere in the world.

End Result: pay less taxes on your hard-earned cash and the only travelling you'll have to do is a short drive to your local ATM and, unlike your current address, it's not 10,000 miles away from home, is it?

Time vs money: the benefits of sound financial planning

Good timing means everything. We live our lives by it, constantly aware of what time it is in order to make our lives run more smoothly. The same principle applies when investing our hard-earned cash.

Time and tide wait for no expatriate. Did you know that the time it takes to double your money in a bank account, assuming a 6% per annum growth, is 12 years. So, if you had a spare 12 or 24 years left to go you'd probably have a tidy sum accumulated. And if you took the time out to deduct a conservative 3% inflation, that sum would only be worth half of its original value. Not funny at all and you're 12 years older! Then, when it's time to go home, that dream house has gone up in price and make no mistake, your local tax inspector will take the time to tax the interest on your hardearned savings.

Ask yourself this question: how many days could you survive on your own assets if you were out of a job – 30, 60, 90 days? Not much more than that, I bet. The amount you need to save should be equal to the amount you can survive on now, in today's money. In other words, you must save on a regular basis what would sustain you if you had to stop work immediately.

Once you have successfully arrived at the amount you need to survive on each week in today's money, add up all your savings and assets and divide the amount by the amount you require to live on each week. For example: If I had $200,000 saved up now and I needed a $2,000 a week to live on, this would last me exactly 100 weeks or only 8.3 years. And I haven't even taken into account inflation, which even at a meagre 5% per annum would ensure that in ten years' time, my $2'000 would only have the spending power of approximately $1180 per week!

Solution: you can make sure you're well prepared for your repatriation or retirement by taking the following steps:

- Take the time to regularly re-evaluate your financial position.
- Aim to provide yourself with another source of income (before you retire).
- Don't rely on bank interest to make you rich or pay the bills, because it won't.
- Invest in an offshore jurisdiction via a good fund manager.
- Aim to be as anonymous as you can within the laws and loopholes that exist (Isle of Man trusts, etc).
- Aim to exceed 20% per annum growth so your money doubles every 4 years and not every 12 years (as in bank interest).
- Take small but calculated risks. Remember, it's your life savings you're dealing with.
- Don't procrastinate. You haven't got the time to waste and putting it off will only compound the problem.

- Make time work for you and not the other way around for a change.
- Plan to make your full-time job a part-time job or even a hobby long before retirement.

Can you pass the button on your own hard-earned cash?

With so many investment options available today, even with technology at our fingertips, it still remains and always will remain down to you as the individual investor to make a final decision on where to place your bets. Like most people, you may have some free time and some spare cash to invest. You will probably take full advantage of surfing the net for instant access to world stock market prices and investment recommendations from one news wire to another. They will tell you, for instance, what is a strong buy, a hold, or a must sell. They will also give you access to information on individual shares and their performance, including the 52-weeks highs and lows of each stock price, earnings ratios, moving averages and of course, a whole host of new IPO listings, together with worldwide economic reports and data.

You may even have a whole host of financial investment sites already book-marked on your computer at home or at the office.

By now, many of you may also have your own e-commerce trading account, ready to buy or sell on the worldwide stock markets at the push of a button. With all this technology at your fingertips and some diligent after-hours research you are able to arrive at a shortlist of a few self-chosen stocks or shares you fancy a dabble at.

Finally, after all those hours of thought you are ready to make a decision. Now, all you have to do is press the button and execute the purchase of your chosen stocks or shares.

But suddenly you freeze. You can't press the button on your own hard-earned cash. You procrastinate and say to yourself or your partner, 'Okay, let's do it tomorrow.' But of course, as you and I both know from past experience, tomorrow never comes. Don't despair, you are not alone! Millions of people are in the same boat. When it comes to the crunch they simply can't press that button when it comes to risking their own money. Call it human nature, or just normal plain old fear, we are all very hesitant when faced with activating what could be a potential selfdestruct button on your own financial well-being. After all, we're not machines, are we? Instead, we all need some sound advice and reassurance from a reliable source before making any important decisions about our financial security. If in any doubt, seek professional advice.

Offshore unit trusts, mutual funds and regular savings: take the worry out of timing when investing

Economic stability and growth should signal the perfect time to invest in the markets – or does it? Always beware of the 'have I missed the boat' approach. Anytime the markets hit new highs, investors inevitably face a nerveracking decision about whether to get in, get out, stay put or invest more?

However, investors can be freed from these stressful decisions by simply investing a portion of their funds in unit trusts or offshore mutual funds, rather than picking a specific day from which the market will rise or fall. Despite what some stockbrokers and financial writers may say to the contrary, any day you pick to invest in a handful of shares you still run the risk that one of the companies you invested in will drop badly and totally offset any gains made in your other shares. Therefore, offshore unit trust typically invests in more than 100 companies, which offers safety in diversification and an easy way to avoid choosing when to invest.

Let's face facts. Stock markets are driven by the outlook for company earnings which, in turn, are affected by economic and political swings. Clearly, all these variables and conflicting professional opinions and predictions can be extremely unnerving to say the least. Take for example the stock market crash of October 1987. If you had invested at the beginning of that year, you would have still finished the year up by 3% ahead of the banks. So, investing the same amount each month (as opposed to a lump sum) greatly reduces the risk of investing when the market is very high. If the market should fall tomorrow, you would have invested only a portion at today's high prices, while next month you invest at a lower price. Alternatively, if the market continues to forge ahead you benefit from its growth.

Always remember that investing via regular monthly instalments host of important, yet imponderable economic factors such as a new budget, the future path of interest rates or the effects of regional and international government trade deficits. In my 25 years of studying and investing in the markets, I have always found there was a divergence of opinion, even amongst the world's top bankers, fund managers and economists, whose views /I regularly keep in touch with. After all, if everyone could predict the future we would all be millionaires!

Dollar cost averaging: how to make money in a volatile stock market

We all remember the basic logic behind Einstein's theory of relativity E-mc2 or Newton's universal law of motion and gravity: that what goes up must come down. Well, the same rules apply to all other things in life. We rudely find this out when we pass the age of 40! However, volatility creates activity and activity creates wealth.

One of my good friends, a precious-metals trader, once told my about hoe he made his money. He illustrated this point on the back of a beer mat. He drew two horizontal lines across the bottom of the beer mat. The top line represented gold and bottom-line silver. He said, 'Mike, if silver followed gold like this on a horizontal line I wouldn't make any money and I'd be out of a job.' I didn't get it. 'What on earth are you talking about?' By way of explanation he drew two more lines underneath the first two, this time not straight but wavy. 'This is how I make my money, Mike. No volatility means no growth, and I can't make any money without it.'

Sometime later I came across an orphan client (don't get me wrong, he did have parents and they were both alive and well). An 'orphan client' is just a term used in the money business when we met a potential client who, for some reason or other, has lost contact with his broker. This guy's name was Geoffrey. He explained that he had recently started two investments – a lump sum and a regular savings plan of a set amount of cash each month. He had started both plans at the same time (approximately 8 months ago). He asked me to check up on how both plans were performing, which of course I was happy to do. When I got the results, I found to my amazement that the regular amount he was saving each month had easily outPerformed the lump sum. A not just by a small amount. In fact, by a staggering 49%!

How can this be?

Both the lump sum and the regular plan were invested in exactly the same funds. So, I decided to investigate further and came up with the following explanation: Geoff had invested a lump sum of US424,000 into an offshore bond. He also decided to invest US43,000 per month into the same funds via a monthly arrangement into a regular savings plan. This was paid from his bank account directly into his savings plan each month. By the time I met Geoff, both his lump sum and the regular plan had amounted to exactly the same in dollar terms, i.e., US43,000 x 8 months = us424,000 or the same as his initial lump sum investment. However, his regular savings plan was now worth US446,500 and his lump sum a mere US$36,000 (US$10,500 less than the regular plan). To illustrate the mechanics of this phenomenon, refer to the graph that follows.

With his lump sum, Geoff purchased 24,000 shares back in March 2000 on a new issue at US$1 each. These shares, when multiplied by the April market slump. These shares, when multiplied by the November bib price of US$1.5 totalled US$36,000. Thereby making him US$12,000 or 5% better off. He was very happy with this.

However, he was even happier when he saw the results of his regular investment. Via this plan, each month when he paid in US$3,000 ha was able to buy a total number of units equal to 31,000 shares (see graph). He did not pay in any more or any less because the price of the shares was fluctuating. Consequently, as his share price tumbled in April and June, his US$3,000 managed months. Once purchased, these shares could not be taken from him. The total amount of shares he accumulated over the past 8 months on his regular savings plan equalled 31,000 shares. When multiplied by the current price of US$1.50 (the same as his lump sum, as they were invested in exactly the same funds) it amounted to US$46,500. If you subtract the total amount of his contributions you will see that he has made a nice profit of US$22,500 or 93.7%!

So, based on these figures, the regular amount he was saving each month clearly out-performed his lump sum by a whopping US$10,500 in only 8 months.

We all know how volatile the stock markets have been of late especially last year (200). Who knows what's around the corner or indeed what next will bring us?

As you can imagine, Geoff is indeed a very happy man. He now doesn't frown so much when the price of his shares goes down, as he knows that thanks to dollar cost averaging his regular contribution will automatically be buying more shares for his money than it did

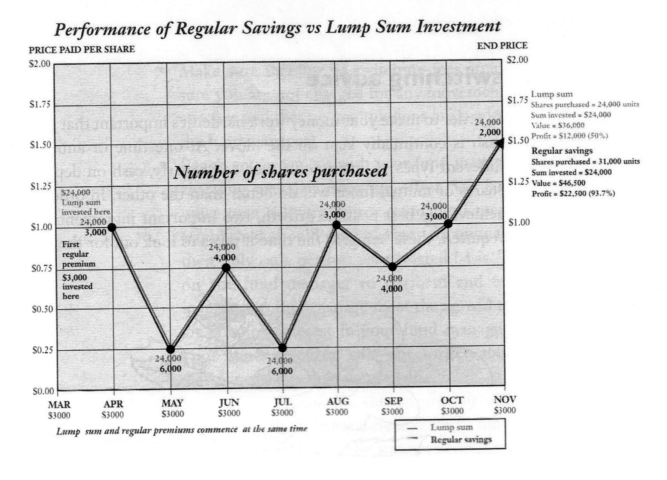

Performance of Regular Savings vs Lump Sum Investment

Lump sum and regular premiums commence at the same time

last month when they were up. And he intends to keep on buying more every month! With this kind of performance, I agree with him entirely.

This method of saving clearly demonstrates how to make money from a volatile or fluctuating stock market. It also relieves the worry and pressure associated with deciding when it's the best time to invest a lump sum. Both methods of saving actually complement each other, as the regular savings plan will keep on performing when the markets fluctuate and diminish the value of the lump sum. A good idea is to start with a lump sum and add to it via a regular savings plan, for what you lose on the round-about you can always gain on the swings.

No growth, no fee: keep your investments on the move with free switching advice

In order to make your money work harder it's important that your cash is continually kept on the move. At one time or another, different types of investments such as property, cash on deposit, shares or mutual funds will do better than the other. In order to achieve the best

possible growth, two important ingredients are required, these being: a) the time it takes to look out for the best

Possible buys and b) The best possible fund manager to invest your cash.

The following tips may help you when making an investment:

- Make sure that there are no up-front charges or loading when you invest.
- Make sure that are there are no switching fees attached (that is, make sure you are not charged for any movement from one fund to another and that no commissions are made on this process by the fund manager).
- Reach an agreement with your fund manager on a reasonable charging structure from the offset, We know that he or she must earn a living, but a good fund manager who is well established should only charge you annually, in arrears, and then only on a performance-related basis. This puts the onus on the fund manager to perform and ensure that all the investments they manage meet the agreed target. Also, having an ongoing interest in your fund management ensures that your fund manager will not forget about you, as many travelling salespeople seem to do.

- A good fund manager should provide you with a monthly report on what is happening and which funds you are invested in, together with a regular statement detailing exactly what you are worth.
- Ask your prospective fund manager about his or her performance track record.
- A fund manager who has done a good job for other people will also have some testimonials (references) from other investors, both locally and globally, who are happy with the performance and after-sales service. A good fund manager should not only supply these but also give you the opportunity to contact other investors to see if they are still happy with the service they are receiving.
- Lastly, take your time and don't forget to shop around. Remember, you've worked very hard for your money, now it's time to make it work hard for you.

The Future-invest in technology

Don't be afraid to try something new with a portion of your savings. Our history books tell us that when technology started to take off, a well-known Scottish inventor, Alexander Graham Bell, created what he thought was a better way of communicating for the future – the telephone. Admittedly not very reliable at first, it's now something that we use every day. I remember reading an old journal entry about scepticism surrounding this particular invention. When this new machine, the telephone, was placed on the desk of an important bank manager, he screamed at his secretary: Please remove this from my desk immediately and bring me my messenger boy!

Now we have the internet and companies like Microsoft, Apple, Oracle, Cisco Systems and Intel to invest in. The new broadband communication systems are now online and it won't be long till we are all communicating via videophone. I also see the future of online broking, currently available on an execution-only basis, consisting of you will be making video calls directly to your broker and 50% technical input and 50% human input. Via the internet, taking active advice while looking at the figures on the same screen, eventually maybe even on your wristwatch.

The handshakes can come later. In fact my last dozen or so clients have come from different parts of the planet and have all found me via my web site: Granddads Investments.com. They have either been referred by existing clients or found the site themselves. I have never met them and probably never will. So, it's true what they say – we now live in a global village. Furthermore, I believe we will be rewarded in the future by becoming a cashless society and exchanging information for goods and services. All future statements, transactions and purchases will be paperless and we will be receiving details of profits in our very own living rooms.

A MODEL PORTFOLIO

Now that we've discussed all the traps and their solutions, here's how to put it altogether in a working model.

Your investment options

Your model portfolio may contain any of the following investments. The key to success is homework and good management. Seek expert advice on buying quality or rarity at the right price. It's also about timing – knowing when to buy and when to sell and move onto the next one. Starting with cash in the bank, these investments are:

- stocks and shares (in old and new economies)

- bonds

- land

- term deposits

- insurance or endowment policies

- savings or pension plans

- precious stones

- technology and telecommunications
- vintage wines

- vintage cars

- works of art

- forestry

- rare stamps or coins

- antiques

- oil and gas

• winning the lottery or gambling

Ask yourself, which of these you currently have or intend to buy in the future?

Economic cyclical movements

Generally speaking, if a country's economy overheats this means that there is more money on the streets. Prices will go up and inevitably so will inflation. Aware of this, the governments of the world step in and increase interest rates in order to stem the growth, reduce domestic debt and stamp out inflation. This is followed by an inevitable credit squeeze. The money comes in off the streets back into the banks and into the government coffers. If there is no inflation on the horizon, interest rates will come down and the stock markets will do well, especially tech stocks (which unlike the old economy do not rely on oil to produce the goods).

When putting together your model portfolio, it's a good idea to keep an eye on the following three indexes:

- Interest rates (borrowing costs)
- Inflation figures (retail price index)
- Oil prices (fuel and energy costs)

These indicators can be your best friend or your worst enemy when designing your model portfolio, for they are the leading signposts that will help you to make or indeed lose money.

What can your portfolio make?

So, how much profit should an ideal portfolio provide? At one time or another, one or more of your individual investments will do better than another. For example, if your property portfolio is doing exceptionally well in a current housing boom, this may be because interest rates are low, therefore people have more confidence to borrow money. Generally speaking, if interest rates are low this is because the economy is not overheating and inflation is being kept in check.

In a bull market, when interest rates are low, inflation is in check and energy costs are affordable, your portfolio should compound at between 15% and 20% per annum.

In a bear market, when supply and demand for goods is low, consumer spending and business confidence are both at a low ebb and the demand for goods is low due to high stockpiles, your portfolio should grow at between 5% and 8% per annum.

The only two situations which fall outside these economic movements are the dreaded recession and depression (as in the 1930's). However, I do not believe this will re-occur in the near future as all the fundamentals are in place to prevent it from happening.

The ideal portfolio

So, without any further delay, what exactly is the ideal investment portfolio?

The simple answer is that there is no easy or correct formula, and it tends to change dramatically depending on where you reside and what stage of life you're at.

Take Singapore for instance, where the ideal financial portfolio consists of what is commonly known as the 5 C's: cash, credit card, car, club membership and condominium.

Whilst in Saudi Arabia, I hear its hip to own an oil well or two, when it comes to expatriates, who come from many diverse backgrounds and are headed in different directions, defining the ideal portfolio is not so simple. Let's look at the basic fundamentals. We all know that we are not going to get rich from interest earned in a bank account. And, as we have seen, the opportunities for investment are numerous. Yet, after all these years of talking to thousands of people from different walks of life, I believe the ideal portfolio is the one you are most happy and relaxed about. The last thing you need when living in a foreign environment is to be stressed out about money.

Your attitude towards risk

So, before leaping ahead, it's important to complete your own self-assessment of your attitude towards risk, that is, whether you wish to take a cautious, balanced or aggressive approach to your investments.

It's a well-known fact that hard-earned cash will do well in the place it is felt most welcome. When putting together your model portfolio, I believe it is important to include a little bit of everything and never get too greedy or take too many risks. After all, it took you a lot of hard work to earn it. Try to watch out for all the traps mentioned in the earlier chapters and remember, nothing lasts forever. So, during your expatriate stint try not to get carried away with overspending. One day your contract will come to an end and so will the extra income.

ever since. It was one of the best pieces of advice I've ever been given.

As for the concept of retirement, that has been replaced by the term 'active retirement,' whereby people will always be doing something to maintain an interest in life and actively manage what they have already accumulated during their working lifetime.

And once you have put together your model portfolio, relax and take some time out for a holiday, because you have worked hard for it and deserve it. But always remember, your money can never take a holiday, to get results it must be at work all the time.

About Granddad Investments....

Granddad Investments provides personal financial services specifically tailored for expatriates. As managing director, I believe that there is no "one-size fits all," portfolio for expatriates. Each individual client's circumstances and requirements are special. Therefore, we make it our priority to take into consideration our clients' financial needs and ambitions (short and long term). The name of the game is to custom build the portfolio around the clint's individual needs. We do this by first assessing our clint's situation and their attitude towards risk or risk adverse investment strategies. This may result in a portfolio based on a cautious, balanced or aggressive approach, or a combination of all three. We then approach the marketplace to find the appropriate investment that each client is happy with. I am a firm believer in maintaining regular contact with existing clients so they are fully aware of what is going on and I'm aware of their ever-changing circumstances. Just like the markets, people's individual needs also change. And that's where good after sales service comes into play.

Over the years I have found that the best way to create a client's ideal portfolio is firstly to communicate with the individual and find out 'where it hurts' – financially speaking of course. It costs them nothing and they are under no obligation to act upon any of the advice that is given. The only way to do business with people, especially when it concerns their finances, is to be truthful and straightforward.

As an investment advisor, you also have to be aware of what is going on the markets and have an understanding of where the money is moving. And thanks to technology, wherever I am on the planet, I am always wired to what is happening on a daily basis.

The Expat Survival Kit – Information Pack

I have put together an information pack that provides you, as an expatriate and potential investor, with the all information you need to start to plan your own ideal investment portfolio. It contains detailed information about how to accumulate a tax – free, anonymous nest egg, together with a Visa/debit card for easy access to your cash via 20 million automatic teller machines world-wide. Also, samples of some leading, tried and tested regular savings, pension and lump sum investment plans that we currently recommend to our clients.

The information pack is free and available via registration on our web site at: **MikeReynard@ outlook.com Or grandadsinvestments@gmail.com** is continually updated with handy new investment tips and up-to-date investment information, as well as background information on our company services and fund management performance, including a copy of our:

- List of services
- Current client newsletter
- Brochure from the Isle of Man government
- Managed Savings Account from all the top overseas institutions (regular and lump sum payments)
- Managed Pension Account from all the top financial institutions (regular and lump sum payments)
- Managed Capital Account from the leading offshore financial institutions) lump sum payments from)
- List of over 200 funds to choose from
- Copy of "live" account statements of existing clients (names and addresses omitted)
- Set of testimonials/references from clients who now live all over the planet. Please feel free to contact any of them to ask their opinion of our service via email or telephone.

- Offshore bank brochure and application form for a deposit account with Visa/ATM/ debit card facilities • Editorial comment from regional press, i.e. The Financial Post (Singapore), The Expat Magazine, Straights Lawyer and other local financial journals

It is my pleasure to offer you only the best services and products on the market. Contact me via my e-mail address. MikeReynard@outlook.com

Lastly, don't worry if you don't get rich, after all it's only money!

Happy investing!

Mike Reynard

LIST OF SERVICES

OFFSHORE BANK ACCOUNTS & VISA GOLD/DEBIT CARDS

This is a vital service which allows you to take full advantage of the many offshore jurisdictions that are classed as tax havens and maintain an essential link to your investment nest egg. We will assist you to open a single or multi-currency account with a free Visa Gold/debit card facility, thereby giving you easy access to your cash, in any local currency, via the world-wide network of 20 million Visa/Delt/Cirrus automatic teller machines. You can implement transactions via telephone and facsimile instructions, direct and instant, thereby effectively cutting the paper trail to the taxman.

OFFSHORE SAVINGS PLANS

Also an essential part of the expatriate savings profile. We will advise you on the best available offshore savings plan to suit your financial goals. After assessing your requirements and attitude to risk, we will look at what's available in the market place and advise you which plan to consider. We will also propose which funds you should invest in (equity and currency based) according to whether you are risk adverse or prefer to take a gamble. We mainly advise on short-term savings plans that can be rolled over at the end of the term, free of any charges. The usual term is 3 to 5 years maximum, which fits in nicely with the length of most expatriate contracts.

OFFSHORE PORTABLE PENSION SCHEMES

Like many expatriates you may have a gap in your pension provision because you cannot contribute to your home-based plan while you are a non-resident working abroad. So why not have your own offshore portable pension plan which travels with you wherever you go? This way you are not leaving any benefits behind. Instead, you are accumulating a solid cash base offshore to provide for your retirement at age 55 or 60.

LUMPSUM INVESTMENTS (GBP, USD, AND ECU)

You are unhappy with current bank interest rates and worried about the effects of inflation on your hard- earned savings, capital gains tax and the government's prying eyes. At Granddad's Investments we provide the following advice free of charge:

A. Thoroughly assess your attitude towards risk and assist you in choosing your initial fund allocation.

B. Select a fund manager via a financial institution (which we propose but is ultimately of your choice).

C. Help you choose the correct terms and conditions of your preferred type of investment i.e. to provide growth or income, or both.

SCHOOL FEES PLANNING

We will assist you in selecting the best savings plan for your children's educational needs. We take into consideration your child's age and the years to go prior to your preferred entry level and are up to date with all the proposal fees, from prep school through to university.

ACTIVE FUND MANAGEMENT SERVICE

You can delegate authority to us to monitor and actively manage your fund portfolio. With this arrangement, we can switch between the available funds on your behalf. No commission is made on the switching. It is free and unlimited bid to bid. We only get paid for results! You pay us only once a year, annually in arrears, and only if we make you a minimum of 10% net growth per annum. Then you pay 1% per annum of the total funds under management. This is an excellent facility for clients who don't have the time or inclination to monitor their investments and fund choice.

TAX ADVICE UPON REPATRIATION

What's the point in accumulating a solid cash base offshore if you have to pay gains tax to your government when you repatriate? Tax advice before and upon repatriation is an essential part of expatriate financial planning.

OFFSHORE SAVINGS PLANS

OFFSHORE TRUSTS @OFFSHORE COMPANY FORMATION

Printed in the United States
by Baker & Taylor Publisher Services